KETTLE WORKOUT

Learn to Build a Strong, Shredded and Functional Body

(The Ultimate Kettlebell Workout to Lose Weight Using Simple Techniques)

Chester Guth

Published by Tomas Edwards

Kettlebell Workout: Learn to Build a Strong, Shredded and Functional Body (The Ultimate Kettlebell Workout to Lose Weight Using Simple Techniques)

ISBN 978-1-990268-61-8

Legal & Disclaimer

The information contained in this book is not designed to replace or take the place of any form of medicine or professional medical advice. The information in this book has been provided for educational and entertainment purposes only.

The information contained in this book has been compiled from sources deemed reliable, and it is accurate to the best of the Author's knowledge; however, the Author cannot guarantee its accuracy and validity and cannot be held liable for any errors or omissions. Changes are periodically made to this book. You must consult your doctor or get professional medical advice before using any of the suggested remedies, techniques, or information in this book.

Table of Contents

Introduction

After many years of working out using conventional methods, I became stuck in routines that bored me and really didn't help me make gains. This all changed when I started changing up my workout methods, so that I could keep my muscles guessing.

One thing that I did was to incorporate kettlebells into my weekly routine.

What you are going to learn about in this guide has been an interest of mine for quite a while, for several reasons. One reason why I was so intrigued by kettlebells is because a lot of people recommended them to me, but I never used them until recently. I always kept putting them off, but I'm glad I decided to change that.

Another reason why I wanted to try using kettlebells was because I had heard that they help shoulder injuries and pain. At the time my right shoulder had some pain, especially when I worked out with heavy weight. So I really wanted something that could correct this.

In this guide you will learn exactly how kettlebells will benefit you, how to choose the right kettlebells that you can workout with, the best exercises that I have found to be the most effective, and several different workouts that you can use.

I thought I'd first start off with some of the benefits you can get from kettlebells.

Chapter 1: What Is Kettlebell Training?

You may be wondering, "What the hell is a kettlebell?" Well, these are weights that are made from cast iron that weigh from 5 pounds to 100 pounds. What makes these weights unique is that they're shaped like a ball that has handles that allow for easier gripping.

Kettlebells originally came from Russia and became popular in the United States only several decades ago. But these days, kettlebells have started to enjoy a renewed popularity thanks largely to a plethora of books, videos, and classes on how to use it. And why all the buzz about it lately? These uniquely shaped exercise tools offer users a unique kind of dynamic weight training that practically targets all essential aspects of being fit: cardiovascular endurance, agility, balance, strength and endurance. And many people love training with kettlebells because of the exercise efficiency it provides (hey, you just need one piece of weight-lifting equipment) and the challenge it provides.

Using Kettlebells

You can use kettlebells by holding them with either one or two hands while doing a wide variety of exercises using different movements. In some, you'll have to shift hands while moving the weight vertically or horizontally, which requires that you engage your core and stabilize your body in ways you've never done with conventional weight or resistance training. Yet, in some, you will need to enlist the power of your hips and legs to move the weight around and, in doing so, give you the chance to perform whole body movements that make many of your muscles work together in ways that they didn't get to in the other resistance training exercises you've done in the past.

Of Kettlebells and Dumbbells

I suspect you may be thinking that kettlebells are practically just dumbbells.

In some ways, they are like dumbbells because they're weights that you can hold with just one hand. But that's where the similarities end. First off, kettlebells are shaped much differently, in case you haven't noticed. Secondly, their unique shape provides it with a much different handle than dumbbells, which drastically changes the weights interact with your muscles.

Yes, the handles do make a big difference. When you use a dumbbell, the weight's gravitational center is inside your hand, i.e., the palm. But with kettlebells, it lies outside of it and that can shift depending on the way you move the weight and how you hold it.

And because of the handles, kettlebell training utilizes momentum, which most traditional strength training movements eschew or consider as taboo. It also produces centrifugal force and together with momentum, trains stabilizing and decelerating muscles much more than traditional resistance-training exercises do. By utilizing training that involves different directions (multi-directional) that recreates many different movements used in real life situations like swinging your luggage so you can store it in an overhead space such as an overhead luggage bin in an airplane.

While you can use dumbbells for effective strength and muscle building using controlled and slow movements, many of which isolate certain muscles, you can use kettlebells to work your muscles in ways that dumbbells can't or shouldn't be used, i.e., using entire body movements that involve dynamic, powerful, and endurance movements.

Why Kettlebells?

Kettlebell training has a myriad number of other benefits, which include:

− First reason is because it's effective in terms of developing core strength, balance, and endurance. This was validated by an 8-week study by the American Council on Exercise. Their researches found that after making their subjects go through 8 weeks of kettlebell training, they noticed substantial improvements in the 3 above mentioned aspects of fitness. And the most significant improvement registered was core strength, which improved by as much as 70%.

– Better agility and muscle coordination.

– Improved body alignment and posture as many kettlebell exercises provide functional training for many postural muscles.

– Efficiency – because you can train multiple muscles and fitness aspects (endurance, power, stability, strength, balance, and cardio) in one workout, you can save time while getting a lot of training done.

– Improved overall functional strength and higher bone density as kettlebell exercises are those that are functional and weight bearing.

– Improved efficiency in terms of performing other exercises.

– Better performance in other sports activities due to increased endurance and power.

– Reduced risk for athletic injuries. Fast stop-and-go sports movements – such as in basketball, football, and tennis, among others – put many poorly conditioned athletes at risk for injuries due to the eccentric nature of deceleration. Because kettlebell exercises help train the body in terms of eccentric deceleration among others, it can train the body in ways that strengthen it to minimize risks for injuries in sports activities.

– A healthier back. Because kettlebell training provides unique patterns of weight loading that isn't available with most traditional weight or resistance training exercises, the lower back muscles are activated in ways that enhance their health, strength, and ability to function.

- Simplicity. While you may need to use different amounts of weights, you only need one kind of equipment – kettlebells. Also, the exercises performed under a kettlebell training program are very simple and straightforward.

For Serious Consideration

While kettlebell training is a very good and efficient way to get into seriously shredded shape, it's not perfect. No training program is. In particular, it can be very challenging for beginners. In order to swing a kettlebell using proper form, a strong physical foundation – a strong core and powerful balance – is required prior to using heavy kettlebell weights. But beginners can perform the most basic and simplest exercises at first to help develop such strength and balance, such as squats, rows, and deadlifts.

Another thing that needs to be taken into consideration is that using kettlebells effectively requires practice and training. The secret to effective kettlebell training is using weights that are heavy enough that you'll need to utilize your legs and hips' power to assist your other muscles in swinging or pushing the weights up. If you're not well-trained to use excellent form, it's very easy to injure your back. As a beginner, it's best to start with lightweights first, seek an expert's assistance in learning to use proper form, or both.

Lastly, because of the unique movements involved in lifting weights during kettlebell training, the risk for injuries are much higher compared to other resistance training programs. These risks however, can be minimized by learning to do the movements right. That's why for the more dynamic kettlebell movements, excellent form is crucial.

The best way to start kettlebell training – aside from reading this book and applying the knowledge gleaned from it – is to make sure you use proper form. For that, it's best to have another person – particularly one who's very familiar with kettlebell training – to give you feedback as to whether or not you're using excellent form. Or you can start by doing the exercises in front of a mirror or recording yourself on video so you can review your executions later on.

Chapter 2: Using The Russian Kettlebell To Get In Shape

The kettlebell, which originated from Russia, is one of the most effective exercise tools to have in your home or office. Many workout gurus claim that you can achieve all of your fitness goals using this simple and cheap workout tool. This book doesn't just claim that; we will also teach you how to do it.

Before we go to the specific workout moves that you can do, let us first discuss why you should choose using the kettlebell instead of the other workout contraptions that you see in TV ads.

It's cheap

One of the most basic sources of appeal for the kettlebell is its low price. The kettlebell that you have today will last for the rest of your life. Unlike the workout machines that you find in gyms, it will not break or malfunction. Good quality kettlebells also don't rust. That means that they will be in good condition even when you've dripped sweat on them for a decade.

It's convenient to use and store

Unlike dumbbells and barbells, you don't have to change the weights in your kettlebell every time you change your exercise move. Each kettlebell has a specific weight. This means that you can immediately pick them up on your workout schedules and start pumping iron. Because you no longer have to deal with iron plates, you will have an easier time putting them away after each workout.

It can be used to work out your whole body

Many people think that kettlebells are the same as ordinary dumbbells. As you explore more of this book however, you will realize that the moves that you can do with kettlebells are a lot more diverse compared to dumbbells. You will be able to use kettlebells not only in strength training but also in improving your cardio-respiratory fitness. The exercises that use kettlebells also make use of more muscle groups compared to the common workout moves performed with barbells. The latter is mostly used in isolating muscle groups. With kettlebells, you have the choice to isolate one muscle group or work on multiple muscle groups simultaneously.

Its ergonomic design mimics carrying everyday objects

We normally carry the kettle ball in the same way we carry plastics of groceries or a briefcase. The wrist position and the suspended arms used when carrying kettle actually allows us to work on the same muscle movements that we execute everyday when we are doing everyday tasks. Using kettlebell will make us stronger in our everyday tasks. This is the reason why both men and women should start using kettlebells in their daily *workout routines.*

Chapter 3: Getting Stronger Without Adding Muscle

Generally the focus of strength training is simply to add more muscle, thereby becoming stronger. This is the equivalent of adding more cylinders to a car engine, rather than fine-tuning the number of cylinders it already has. When you are exercising one muscle, you can create more power and strength by recruiting the surrounding muscles into the exercise. This is known as Irradiation. An example of this would be bicep curls, as when you reach the point at which you think you cannot do another rep, simply squeeze the handle of the dumbbell as hard as you can and you'll find that you can manage another rep or two.

The same idea applies with pull-ups and squats. If you concentrate on squeezing your abs and glutes, this will enable you to manage an additional few reps. Essentially this is 'loading' your muscle prior to using it, which actually increases the amount of muscle fiber in the key muscle that you will recruit. Once you begin to feel the muscle starting to contract to its maximum level, branch out from that centre to other related muscles. The trick is to maintain tension in as many surrounding muscles as possible.

A way to picture this is to try throwing a hard punch while sitting down with your legs folded - you'll soon find strong arms aren't worth much if you can't incorporate the rest of your body. While it may appear obvious with the example above, there are numerous exercises where it is not obvious at all and yet works surprisingly well. As the saying goes; you can't fire a cannon from a canoe.

Breathing also plays an important role as contrary to popular theory exhaling as you press/pull the weight is not the most effective method. Maintaining internal pressure in your diaphragm is key to keeping your abdomen rock solid and maximising strength output. I'm certainly not saying to hold your breath through the whole movement, just the most taxing points.

Key takeaways:

Boost irradiation via one of three ways:

Squeezing the bar or simply clench your fist as hard as possible.

Tense your abs (not suck in) as hard as you can similar to when you do a plank.

Clench your butt and tighten your sphincter muscle (strange I know).

For breathing hold your breath maintaining internal pressure through the strenuous proportion of the movement and release your breath when lowering the weight.

The easiest way to visualise this idea is a drinking straw and how if you bend the walls of the straw it is quite flimsy, but once they straighten the straw it gains a new level of rigidity similar to your body when you add tension through the above techniques.

6 Reasons to Train with Kettlebells

Kettlebell exercise are functional full body movements: Modern fitness culture has us pounding away on treadmills and using fixed weight machines. These are fine when aiming to achieve aesthetic results, but generally you are only working one plane of movement. This is of little use for sports or movements in the real world, such as lifting boxes, carrying suitcases upstairs and picking up children. Kettlebell training emphasizes movements not muscles whilst allowing for whole-body functional training. It's well known that the compound, whole body movements typical of kettlebell exercises are superior to machines that isolate muscles for improving stability, body composition (through higher calorie burn), and functional strength. Furthermore, kettlebells strengthen the tendons and ligaments, making the joints tougher and less susceptible to injury.

Kettlebells are addictive: High rep sets of kettlebell swings, snatches and squats all have a nice rhythm to them and are satisfying. They also enable quick workouts, as with compound muscle movements a workout shouldn't exceed 30-40 minutes. I find that I enjoy using them because I'm able to stick to the workouts and achieve consistent results.

Great for fat loss: Due to the explosive and full body movement of kettlebells, there is a high metabolic cost of lifting, pressing and pulling the kettlebell. Most high rep kettlebell exercises will out-strip straight cardio exercises such as running and cycling, even before taking into account the afterburn effect. Building lean muscle also adds to your calorie furnace, helping to lift your resting metabolism for prolonged periods.

Inexpensive, compact and portable:Expect to pay approximately $4 dollars per kilogram for a kettlebell, i.e. a 20kg kettlebell should cost you roughly $80. This is incredibly affordable when you consider their versatility, effectiveness, and the fact they don't take up any space to store. When trying to fit cardio, strength and flexibility training into an already overbooked schedule, kettlebells can produce surprising results, even after only 15-30minute workouts. Being so small and portable, training can take place in your bedroom, backyard, local park, beach or pretty much anywhere with a bit of open space.

Minimalist Training:There is a lot to be said for keeping your training simple and short. I always smile when seeing someone work through an exercise program of machine hamstring curls, calf raises, leg press and hip abductors, instead of hitting them all in one movement via the kettlebell swing. Plus get the bonus of a good dose of cardio, rather than resting between all the isolation exercises. Gone are the days of splitting cardio and strength training, since Kettlebells combine cardio and strength training effectively and conveniently.

Build your posterior:Kettlebell movements are not isolation or single joint movements, as every swing, lift or press recruits many joints and muscle groups. This aids the body to always work as a one, the glutes and the hard-to-hit hip flexor muscles are targeted in kettlebell training. Not utilising your glutes when you lift or extend your hips can cause your lower back to over compensate, resulting in lower back pain and injuries. The lower back muscles were never intended to do the job of your glutes, which are a far larger muscle. Teaching your body a more correct, fluid movement pattern boosts your functionality and helps to correct any muscular imbalances you may have. Kettlebells strengthen the entire posterior chain, which not only assists athletic performance but also builds solid posture that helps to showcase all your hard work. Since most kettlebell exercises can be performed with a single limb, you will naturally even out your musculature, ensuring that both sides of your body are equally functional.

Improve your balance and coordination: The structure of the kettlebell naturally builds balance and coordination, as the weight is off-centre, thereby forcing your body to constantly stabilise it. Training with a single kettlebell or on one leg improves balance, ankle strength, and knee stability; while also working your core.

Chapter 4: Warm Up And Cool Down

Warm up and cool down

Warming up is very important before starting any excise and kettlebell training is no exception to this. One should warm up correctly to avoid muscle injuries. Mobility is key in any workout. Keeping your joints mobile ensures movement without compensation while reducing the chances of getting injured. This keeps your joints strong and healthy. A good warm-up program should not only ready you physically but also mentally and neurologically because the body needs to be turned on ready for action.

The joints to focus on include

Neck – cervical spine

Shoulders – both shoulder capsule and girdle

Upper back – thoracic spine

Wrist and elbows

Upper pelvis

Lower pelvis

Knees and ankles

While many of the warm-up activities offer circulation mobility and joint preparation they focus mainly on the engagement required to move a kettlebell effectively and efficiently.

Around the world

This is done by picking the kettlebell and swinging it around your waistline. You should prioritize moving the kettlebell smoothly and ensure your midline is solid. Undertake this exercise with a light weight so as to achieve smooth movement of the bell through space while maintaining control.

Make sure you maintain a circular kettlebell path and avoid swinging it low across front and back. The midline should be stable with minimal deviation from the vertical standing position. The exercise should be about developing control and mastery of moving the kettlebell through space. Do not shift your weight to accommodate the path of the kettlebell. The kettlebell should never lose its path as it passes from hand to hand. Since your body is intelligent enough to choose the direction that feels more natural and easy you should always try to balance between your dominant and no dominant sides.

Figure eight

This requires a stable and static body and the only movements is that of the arms and the kettlebell. This move warms your legs and hip hinge. You begin in a wide stance and smoothly pass the kettlebell between your legs and around one and back again around the other leg drawing a figure eight.

Halos

It allows one to move and control the kettlebell while maintaining a strong and stable midline. It offers a complete

Chapter 5: Literature Review

We can easily gauge the effectiveness of kettlebell training by the increase in usage in gyms across the world and the positive changes that it has made in the lives of many people. Folks who train with kettlebells have found their strength and power to increase while also having a greater sense of enjoyment because of the uniqueness of training with kettlebells.

But what does the scientific research say about kettlebells? Because of the increasing popularity of kettlebell training, kettlebells have become of the subject of a considerable amount of academic and scientific research. In this chapter, let's move things from the anecdotal to the academic and look at what some of the research is saying. All sources will be linked below.

Increases in maximal and explosive strength

One of the biggest advantages to kettlebell training is that it leads to increases in strength and power simultaneously. We can define strength as the ability to lift or carry a large amount of weight, while power is the ability to move weight with speed. Kettlebell training increases absolute strength and the ability to move an object quickly.

According to research, a program of swing training increased maximal strength by almost 10 percent over 6 weeks while also increasing cardiovascular ability and jumping power. This was measured by testing healthy men before and after 6 weeks on a kettlebell swing program and 6 weeks on a jump squat program. The group of healthy males that performed a biweekly 12-minute swing workout for 6 weeks showed an increase in maximum strength and explosive strength that would point towards an increase in cardiovascular fitness.

The full body movement of the kettlebell swing means that strength and explosive jumping power can be trained simultaneously.

Two other studies showed that kettlebell training increases strength and power, one focusing on young populations and the other focusing on overall strength compared with barbell movements. The latter study was able to show an increase specifically in clean and jerk when using kettlebells as well as a transference of power and strength to traditional and bodyweight training.

A more economical alternative to traditional weight lifting

You don't need to break the bank and turn your entire garage or basement into a gym to get the benefits of weight training. Research suggests that kettlebells are an effective alternative to barbells and machines.

A particular research study conducted in the Journal of Strength and Conditioning Research provides evidence that kettlebells are an effective alternative to traditional weightlifting methods, especially when considering the size, portability and relative low cost of kettlebells as compared with barbells, weight plates, squat racks and benches. A well-formed training plan with kettlebells can lead to the same gains in strength, power and muscular endurance but with less cost and space demand. The study shows that kettlebell training can create the same effects as other, more traditional forms of strength training.

Increase in cardiovascular fitness

Kettlebell training is an effective way to increase your metabolism, vo2 max (the ability for your body to transport oxygen — a higher vo2 max generally means a higher amount of endurance) and burn calories.

One study found that a regimen of simple kettlebell movements created the same "metabolic cost" as fast walking on an inclined treadmill. This means that a workout consisting of, in the case of the study, alternating 10 swings and 10 kettlebell deadlifts conditioned the cardiovascular system to the same level as that of graded treadmill walking. All of this happened with a lower impact and a higher perceived rate of exertion while also increasing heart rate.

Psychological benefits

Another study found that using kettlebells as part of a change to an active lifestyle made for positive overall mental health benefits. To quote from the study, kettlebell training "increased overall well-being, job satisfaction, and self-reported muscular strength that are valuable psychosocial factors and should be considered an alternative to more common strategies [in fitness]".

It is my belief that the creativity and novelty of kettlebell training makes for this psychological benefit. Kettlebell training is fun and feels like a hard workout when it is completed. You may have experienced something similar in your own training, when knowing that you just made it through a difficult workout can give a big mental boost. Effective exercise also helps with the release of chemicals that can ease stress and lead to a positive mental framework.

Tabata training

A popular routine is called Tabata training, and it has been shown in multiple research studies to be an immensely efficient way to burn calories and kick start your metabolism.

The Tabata protocol is named after Dr. Izumi Tabata and was developed in the 1990's as a quick training method for cyclists and speed skaters. It has since exploded in popularity and is being adapted into many different exercise disciplines. One of which is CrossFit, and many CrossFit gyms use the Tabata protocol in workouts.

So what is it? The Tabata protocol is repeating high-intensity intervals. The repeat is built around 8 sets of 20 seconds on 10 seconds off. If you have heard of sprint-interval training (SIC), it has its basis in this Tabata protocol.

The study compared a Tabata protocol kettlebell workout with a sprint-interval (SIC) training workout on a stationary bicycle. The SIC workout involved 30 second, full intensity sprints with 4 minute rest. The Tabata kettlebell workout was built with the 20/10 sequence and went from sumo squats to swings to clean and press to sumo deadlifts.

The study found that the Tabata style workout that involved kettlebell movements lead to a higher VO2 max (your body's ability to produce and utilize oxygen and thus be more able to endure long sustained efforts), calorie burn and positive cardiovascular and metabolic adaptations.

Talk about bang for your buck — by implementing this 4 minute workout into your exercise routine you can kick start your metabolism and build mitochondria strength.

Sources Cited

Lake, Jason P., and Mike A. Lauder. "Kettlebell Swing Training Improves Maximal and Explosive Strength." Journal of Strength and Conditioning Research, vol. 26, no. 8, 2012, pp. 2228–2233.

Spierer, David. "Transference of Kettlebell Training to Strength, Power, and Endurance." Journal of Strength and Conditioning Research, National Strength and Conditioning Association, Feb. 2013.

Jay, Kenneth, et al. Effects of Kettlebell Training on Postural Coordination: The Journal of Strength & Conditioning Research. National Strength and Conditioning Association, 2013.

Thomas, James F., et al. "Comparison of Two-Hand Kettlebell Exercise and Graded Treadmill Walking." Journal of Strength and Conditioning Research, vol. 28, no. 4, 2014, pp. 998–1006.

Manocchia, Pat, et al. "Transference of Kettlebell Training to Traditional Olympic Weight Lifting and Muscular Endurance."

Journal of Strength & Conditioning Research (Lippincott Williams & Wilkins), vol. 24, 02 Jan. 2010.

Girard, Joe and Syed Hussain. "The Effects of Kettlebell Training on Strength, Power, and Endurance." Physical Therapy Reviews, vol. 20, no. 1, Feb. 2015, pp. 8-15.

Williams, Brian M., and Robert R. Kraemer. "Comparison of Cardiorespiratory and Metabolic Responses in Kettlebell High-Intensity Interval Training Versus Sprint Interval Cycling." Journal of Strength and Conditioning Research, vol. 29, no. 12, 2015, pp. 3317–3325.

Andersen, Vidar, et al. "Core Muscle Activation in One-Armed and Two-Armed Kettlebell Swing." Journal of Strength and Conditioning Research, vol. 30, no. 5, 2016, pp. 1196–1204.

Chapter 6: How Often Should Women Exercise With Kettlebells?

How often you train depends on how quickly you recover from your last workout. After each workout, your body needs time to repair the tissue damage and restore balance or homeostasis.

If you do not rest for long enough between workouts, it will result in fatigue, potential injury, and an inability of your muscles to grow in size and shape.

Women, of course, recover faster from the sport than men. Men can be sore for up to 72 hours after training, while women are usually only sore for 24 hours.

However, your body's ability to recover from exercise is influenced by more than just your gender.

• Older

• Quality of nutrition

- Exercise intensity

- Daily activities

- Genetics

- Sporting experience

All these factors affect how quickly you recover from your last workout.

Ultimately, you need to listen to your body, and if you feel tired or discouraged, take you a few days rest.

As a general goal for shorter workouts (see workout below), but more often, 4-5 workouts a week is a good start.

If you feel you can do more, go out and cycle, walk, swim, and stay active.

You should also think about exercise in the long term. Be consistent — train rather than force workouts.

3 Kettlebell Workouts For Women

Here are 3 workouts for getting started.

Go slowly, if you feel sore after training, take a day off.

The target for 4-5 workouts per week

Start with Training 1 and do not continue with Training 2 until you can comfortably complete 3 laps.

WORKOUT 1 - BEGINNER KETTLEBELL WORKOUT FOR WOMEN

• Kettlebell Single Arm Deadlift - 12 reps on each side

• Kettlebell Squat and Press - 12 reps (6 on each side or 12 keep the kettlebell in both hands)

• Kettlebell Row - 12 reps on each side

• Push-Ups - 12 reps (use a table, a staircase, a bench if you want to make it easier)

• Rest 60 seconds and repeat a total of 3 turns

If the Squat and Press is too much, do squats without the press. Remember to focus on the technique and the depth of the squat.

WORKOUT 2 - KETTLEBELL CORE CONDITIONER FOR WOMEN

• Kettlebell Single Leg Deadlift - 6 reps on each side

• Kettlebell Side Lunge - 6 reps on each side

• Kettlebell Squat and Press - 12 reps (6 on each side or 12 keep the kettlebell in both hands)

• Kettlebell Turkish Get Up - 3 on each page

• Rest 60 seconds and repeat a total of 3 turns

This training is much more technical than the first one. There are more demands on the core muscles, balance, and technique. Take your time and do the exercises properly.

WORKOUT 3 - FULL BODY KETTLEBELL TONE AND FAT ATTACK

• Kettlebell Turkish Get Up - 3 repetitions on each page

- Kettlebell Swing - 20 reps

- Kettlebell Side Lunge - 8 repetitions on each side

- Kettlebell Squat and Press - 10 reps on each side

- High knees - 50 reps (run on the spot, lift your knees, count only one leg)

- Rest 60 seconds and repeat a total of 3 turns

Now we're starting to increase that heart rate.

Kettlebells are a great choice for women and very effective. Switching from cardio-based workouts to resistance-based workouts will have a major impact on the female body.

Chapter 7: Safety Tips For Kettlebell Training

Consistency with kettlebell training is the key to losing weight and getting fit quickly. Time spent away from kettlebell training due to wounds, or icing knees, shoulders, and wrists is a waste of time. You can get in shape by spending this time in burning fat of your body and building lean muscles. Therefore, it is best to take some safety measures and not get hurt in order to perform consistently and get quicker results.

Warm Up

Even if you are an advanced lifter and have been training with heavier kettlebells for months and years, it is always a good idea to do some push-ups, light stretching, and a few minutes of cardio before doing ballistic exercises with a heavy kettlebell. It is important to warm up in order to prevent any muscle pull or muscle spasm.

Quick 2 minute kettlebell warm up: https://youtu.be/QSYU-6EwPql

Don't Push Yourself

It is good to set higher targets but do not push yourself to start kettlebell training with a 24kg kettlebell if you are a novice. Proceed step by step, practice with lighter kettlebells first, and master a technique before moving on to heavier kettlebells and intensive movements.

Breathe Properly

Proper breathing is essential for using a kettlebell safely. Concentrate on the technique rather than on the volume of repetitions. If you are doing an intensive movement such as a deadlift to squat thrust and you find yourself exhausted and breathless, take a moment and switch to lighter basic kettlebell movements to catch your breath.

Proper breathing is also important to minimize the pressure on your spine. Abdominal bracing is a technique, which utilizes breathing patterns to tighten the abdominal muscles that in turn protect your spine. Practice this technique to know how you can tighten your abdominal muscles as you exhale.

Eliminate Distractions

Kettlebell training requires focus and concentration. Distractions and interruptions not only decrease the effectiveness of kettlebell training, they increase the risk of injuries too. Focus on your technique and breathing instead of contemplating things that do not matter in that moment.

Choose the Right Size

Your wrong selection of kettlebell not only can hurt you but it can hurt others as well. Kettlebell training is very different from traditional weight lifting and cardio workout. It is wise to get help from an expert in selecting appropriate kettlebell for you. A kettlebell that is too heavy for your strength and ability can lead to an ineffective training session as well as injuries. It is better to start with a lighter kettlebell and master the basic techniques with it before moving up to a heavier kettlebell and intensive movements.

Beware of Your Surroundings

Always ensure that you have enough room around you to perform the movements without harming other people, objects, or yourself. Kettlebell training involves dynamic movements. Have a clear floor space with no object on the floor to trip over. Stay clear of wall and mirrors and anything else that can be harmed if you lose control of the kettlebell. Do not try to catch the kettlebell if you lose control or drop it during an exercise. Let it drop on the floor. The worst thing that can happen is that you damage the floor.

Learn the Technique

Learning proper kettlebell movements from an experienced instructor is essential. Improper positioning of the body can lead to injuries in the shoulders and back. Maintaining a firm grip on the kettlebell and wearing flat-soled shoes are two important considerations for all types of kettlebell exercises.

Do Not Stop Moving

Once you are done with your kettlebell training, do not stand still or sit down. Walk around the room until your heart rate and breathing normalize. Standing or sitting still immediately after kettlebell training can elevate blood pressure that can cause serious health complications.

Chapter 8: Warming Up

Have you ever skipped a warm-up because it takes up extra time or maybe you just didn't feel like it? Warming up is not just a frivolous activity that can be overlooked before exercise. A warm-up before any form of physical activity, including something as mundane as mowing the lawn, is a vital part of preventing injury. When you warm up properly before an activity, you are preparing your body for what you are about to do. A good warm-up has various benefits that will help you progress in your kettlebell training.

BODY TEMPERATURE

Warming up before a workout will raise your body temperature slightly and warm your muscles. Warm muscles are less stiff and stretch more comfortably. Kettlebell exercises are dynamic and fast-paced, if your muscles aren't sufficiently warmed up, they may not be able to stretch to the limits you are asking them to. This is why getting them warm before physical activity is important to prevent injuries such as muscle strains and tears.

BLOOD FLOW AND OXYGEN

For your muscles to perform optimally, they need blood and oxygen. Warm-ups include a light aerobic aspect which raises your heart rate and breathing. Blood vessels in your body also dilate, allowing the volume of blood being pumped through them to increase. Your heart starts pumping oxygen-rich blood to the various muscles around your body, supplying them with what they need to get ready for action. Bear in mind that your heart is also a muscle and it is the most important muscle in your entire body. When you don't warm up before an activity, unnecessary stress is placed on your heart to work harder and faster without that increased warmth and elasticity of the muscle beforehand.

FLEXIBILITY AND JOINTS

A good warm-up routine consists of both light aerobics or cardio and stretching. The cardio gets your muscles warmed up, blood flowing, and increases your oxygen intake and delivery to your muscles. Once your muscles are warmed up, it's time to stretch them out. Warming them before stretching is important because stretching muscles that are cold and less elastic can cause injuries such as muscle strains. Stretching your muscles out before a workout helps to lengthen them before you work them, providing you with a fuller range of motion than tight, cold muscles would.

Your joints also benefit from a good warm-up session. The fluid found around many of your joints is called synovial fluid. Along with your muscle temperature increasing slightly, the temperature of this joint fluid also goes up. Warm synovial fluid around your joints allows smoother movement. If you go full tilt into a workout without warming the synovial fluid, you could end up experiencing joint pain.

MUSCLE TENSION

Warming up before a workout helps to ease your muscles into the more intense activity. Muscle tension and aches from a previous workout are reduced, allowing them to function better during your workout. If you think that warming up well-rested muscles is important, warming up muscles that are still tense and sore from two days ago is even more crucial.

Tense and sore muscles are more vulnerable to injury during your workout. In addition to preventing injury during a workout, a decent warm-up will also reduce the amount of muscle stiffness and ache after you have finished exercising. In the prevention of muscle ache and stiffness post-exercise, warming up and cooling down work hand-in-hand. You cannot do one and not do the other and expect the same benefits to apply throughout.

RANGE OF MOTION AND PERFORMANCE

When your muscles are warmed up, they contract and relax more quickly and easily. When your joints are warmed up, they move more smoothly with a reduced risk of pain. Your heart experiences less stress when you warm it up and get it ready for exercise. Your blood flow and oxygen intake are increased, providing more blood and oxygen to your muscles before you push them to their limits. All of this helps to increase your flexibility, range of motion, respiration, cardiac output, speed, and strength which are all aspects of boosting your performance during a workout.

RISK OF INJURY

When you warm up, you aren't just warming up your muscles. You are warming up every part of your body that will play a role in your exercise. When your body moves more smoothly, stretches more easily, and performs better, you run less of a risk of causing injury to all the different body parts involved. Types of injuries that may be avoided by warming up properly include:

Muscle strains

Sprains

Muscle tears

Muscle cramps

Joint injuries

Post-workout injuries

Post-workout injuries may occur from performing everyday activities when your muscles have been put through a grueling training session without being suitably warmed up and cooled down. Exercising places strain on your muscles, it's supposed to. You cannot grow muscle without first putting it under pressure and breaking it down.

Muscles are rebuilt stronger and better during the post-exercise recovery period. You place your muscles under additional strain during your workout by not warming up properly. Doing so increases your risk of something small, like lifting a heavy package, acting as the straw that broke the camel's back. That strain on your already taxed muscles could be just that little bit too much for them to handle, allowing them to become injured. Warming up sufficiently can help prevent this from happening.

THE WARM-UP

JOINT MOBILITY WARM-UP EXERCISES

‰ NECK

Neck and shoulder problems affect each other because your neck and shoulder joints are connected to each other. So, warming up your neck is just as important as warming up your shoulders.

Notes regarding your neck warm-up:

It is important not to perform these movements quickly or jerkily; they should be done in a slow, measured, and controlled manner.

Don't overextend the warm-up movements.

Keep your breathing natural and comfortable. Avoid holding your breath in.

Keep your shoulders relaxed in a downward and backward position.

Neck Warm-Up 1: Ear to Shoulder

Stand in a relaxed, neutral position with your feet about shoulder-width apart, shoulders back and down.

Start by looking straight ahead and reach your right arm over the top of your head so that your right hand is touching your left ear.

Slowly and carefully tilt your head sideways, bringing your right ear closer to the top of your right shoulder.

Gently hold your head in that position for approximately 20 seconds. Do not force your neck to overstretch by pushing with your hand.

Release the stretch and return to your original position slowly.

Neck Warm-Up 2: Look Left to Right

Stand in a relaxed, neutral position with your feet about shoulder-width apart, shoulders back and down.

Start by looking straight ahead. Using a slow and controlled movement, look as far to your left as you comfortably can without straining and without moving your torso or shoulders.

Hold this position for two deep breaths before slowly returning to your original position.

Neck Warm-Up 3: Chin Up and Down

Stand in a relaxed, neutral position with your feet about shoulder-width apart, shoulders back and down.

Start by looking straight ahead. Slowly drop your chin so that it comes as close to touching your chest as possible.

Slowly raise your chin towards the ceiling so that your head is tilted as far backwards as possible without discomfort.

Slowly bring your head back to the original position.

Neck Warm-Up 4: Neck Rolls

Stand in a relaxed, neutral position with your feet about shoulder-width apart, shoulders back and down.

Start by looking straight ahead. Slowly bring your chin as close to your chest as possible without straining and roll your head in circles in a clockwise direction.

Swap directions and roll your head slowly in a counterclockwise direction.

‰ SHOULDERS

Your shoulders are powerful and often used during kettlebell workouts whether directly or indirectly. This makes it important to warm them up properly before exercising. If you don't have good mobility in your shoulders, your lower and upper back may try to compensate which could cause an injury from overuse.

An example of a lack of mobility in your shoulders and upper back impacting your performance is seen when you lean backward when trying to hold a kettlebell straight over your head. This results in over-arching your lower back, and ultimately, lower back pain.

Shoulder Warm-Up 1: Backwards and forward Shoulder Circles

Stand in a relaxed, neutral position with your feet about shoulder-width apart, shoulders back and down.

Start with both arms relaxed at your sides. Begin rotating one arm forward in a large circle, rotating from the shoulder, and keeping the arm close to the body.

Change directions to rotate the arm backward in a large circle, rotating from the shoulder and keeping the arm close to the body.

Switch to the other arm and perform the same forward and backward circle rotation of the shoulder.

Shoulder Warm-Up 2: Lasso Overhead

Stand in a relaxed, neutral position with your feet about shoulder-width apart, shoulders back and down.

Start with both arms relaxed at your sides. Raise one arm overhead. Circle your arm in the air in a clockwise direction as if swinging a lasso. Keep the arm as straight as possible during the rotation.

Switch to rotating the lasso motion in a counterclockwise direction, keeping the arm as straight as possible throughout.

Change to the other arm and perform the same exercise, rotating the shoulder in a lasso motion in both clockwise and counterclockwise directions.

Shoulder Warm-Up 3: Inward and Outward Rotations

Stand in a relaxed, neutral position with your feet about shoulder-width apart, shoulders back and down.

Start with both arms relaxed at your sides. Raise one arm sideways to shoulder height until it is parallel to the ground, palm facing downward.

Turn the arm over so that the thumb is facing backwards with the palm facing upwards and the back of the hand is facing downward.

Return the arm to the original position with the palm facing downward again.

Turn the arm in the opposite direction so that the thumb is again facing backwards, palm facing upwards, and back of the hand facing downward.

Switch the other arm and perform the same exercise of turning the arm in both directions.

Shoulder Warm-Up 4: Self-Hugs

Stand in a relaxed, neutral position with your feet about shoulder-width apart, shoulders back and down.

Start with both arms relaxed at your sides.

Swing each arm around your body at chest height so that your hands touch the opposite outer shoulder, as if you were giving yourself a big hug.

You can additionally perform a variation of this exercise by lowering your arms to waist height, swinging your arms so that you are clapping your hands together in front of and behind your body.

Shoulder Warm-Up 5: Shoulder Rolls

Stand in a relaxed, neutral position with your feet about shoulder-width apart, shoulders back and down.

Start with both arms relaxed at your sides.

With both arms still at your sides, pull both shoulders forward and then slowly roll them upwards and backward, bringing them downward and forward again to complete circular motion.

Change direction and repeat.

Try to make the circular roll of your shoulders as large as possible by bringing them as far forward, lifting as high, pulling as far backward, and completing the circle by dropping them as low as possible.

‰ UPPER BACK

Many people exhibit less than ideal mobility of the upper back area. This results from long stretches of sitting at a desk and a lack of movement in general. Improving upper back mobility will prevent the neck, shoulders, and lower back from becoming overused as compensation.

Upper Back Warm-Up 1: Rotations

Stand in a relaxed, neutral position with your feet about shoulder-width apart, shoulders back and down.

Start with both arms relaxed at your sides.

Raise your left arm and bring it around to touch your right outer shoulder.

Bring your right arm around your back, back of the hand facing your back, palm facing outwards.

At the same time, rotate your torso from left to right with your left shoulder moving to the right and rotating your neck so that you are looking over your right shoulder.

Be sure to keep your feet in place and your shoulders down.

Repeat this rotation in the opposite direction, moving from right to left.

Upper Back Warm-Up 2: Lateral Reaches

Stand in a relaxed, neutral position with your feet about shoulder-width apart, shoulders back and down.

Start with both arms relaxed at your sides.

Raise both arms up to shoulder height, parallel to the ground with your palms facing downward.

Keep the hips stationary and lean sideways as far to the left as possible, as if reaching to touch the wall.

Swap sides and reach to the right.

Reach as far sideways as possible in both directions without moving your hips.

Upper Back 3: Opening the Chest

The chest area can become tight with little proper mobility due to spending many hours a day sitting or working on a computer. It is important to open this area so that you can achieve a full range of motion.

Stand in a relaxed, neutral position with your feet about shoulder-width apart, shoulders back and down.

Start with both arms relaxed at your sides, palms facing backwards and backs of the hands facing forward, thumbs pointing inwards towards your body.

Slowly pull your shoulders back and rotate the arms outwards so that the hands rotate until the thumbs are pointing outwards and away from your body.

Slowly bring your shoulders all the way forward and down, rotating the arms inwards so that you end in the starting position.

‰ ELBOWS

You use your elbow joints frequently while performing kettlebell exercises. Poor elbow joint mobility can cause overuse of the wrists and shoulders as compensation.

Elbow Warm-Up 1: Flex and Extend

Stand in a relaxed, neutral position with your feet about shoulder-width apart, shoulders back and down.

Start with both arms relaxed at your sides.

Bend the elbow to 90 degrees, bringing your forearm parallel with the ground.

Raise your elbow upwards towards your ear as if you were reaching for the back of your shoulder blade.

Change to the other arm and perform the same exercise.

This exercise can also be done with both arms simultaneously.

Elbow Warm-Up 2: Elbow Lassos

Stand in a relaxed, neutral position with your feet about shoulder-width apart, shoulders back and down.

Start with both arms relaxed at your sides.

Raise your arm to the side, parallel with the ground and bend the elbow at a 90-degree angle.

Rotate your forearm clockwise in a circular motion, similar to swinging a lasso.

Switch to rotating your forearm in the opposite counterclockwise direction.

Change to your other arm and perform the same exercise.

‰ WRISTS

Working with kettlebells is going to work your wrist joints quite heavily. You may experience poor wrist joint mobility due to numerous hours spent working on a computer daily.

Wrist Warm-Up 1: Rotations, Backwards and forward, Side to Side

Stand in a relaxed, neutral position with your feet about shoulder-width apart, shoulders back and down.

Start with both arms relaxed at your sides.

Raise both arms forward and bend the elbow to 90 degrees. Bring your wrists and forearms together, clasp your hands together, and interlace your fingers.

Roll your wrists in circles, making the circles as big as possible to reap maximum mobility benefits.

Move your wrists side to side or left to right so that the back of each hand is moving towards the outside of your forearm.

Move your wrists backward and forward, thumb towards your chest, and pinky finger forward away from your chest.

Wrist Warm-Up 2: Wrist Extensions

Stand in a relaxed, neutral position with your feet about shoulder-width apart, shoulders back and down.

Start with both arms relaxed at your sides.

Raise both arms forward until they are parallel with the ground, palms facing downward and fingers straight.

Take your left hand and gently pull the fingers of your right hand up and backwards so that your palm is facing forward and slightly upwards. Pull back as far as you can until you can feel the stretch in the inner wrist and forearm without straining.

Using your left hand, gently pull the fingers of your right hand downward and back so that your palm is facing back towards your body and your fingertips are pointing downward. Pull back as far as you can until you can feel the stretch in the outer wrist and forearm without straining.

Swap to your left hand and repeat the exercise.

‰ HIPS

Poor hip mobility can result in excessive and exaggerated lower back and knee movements. This may cause back pain and other back-related problems as well as problems with your knees.

Hip Warm-Up 1: Circles

Stand in a relaxed, neutral position with your feet about shoulder-width apart.

Place your hands on your hips and rotate your hips in a large circle in a clockwise direction, keeping your feet still.

Make the circle as large as you can and ensure that you perform a full circle, don't cut corners.

Change to rotating your hips in a counterclockwise direction.

Hip Warm-Up 2: Side to side, Backwards and forward

Stand in a relaxed, neutral position with your feet about shoulder-width apart.

Place your hands on your hips. Push your right hip out to the right, leaning your torso to the left. Keep your back as straight upright as possible to avoid leaning forward.

Come back to the starting position and repeat to the other side, pushing your left hip out to the left and leaning your torso over to the right.

Come back to the starting position. Push your hips backwards and lean your torso forward, as if sticking your bottom out backwards.

Come back to the starting position again. Push your hips out forward, squeezing your glutes to support your lower back.

Hip Warm-Up 3: Leg Circles

Stand in a relaxed, neutral position with your feet about shoulder-width apart.

Stand on one leg and raise the other leg slightly outwards to the side, keeping your leg as straight as possible.

Rotate your leg in a circular motion in a clockwise direction as if drawing circles with your foot.

Change direction to rotate your leg in circles in a counterclockwise direction.

Switch legs to perform the exercise with the other leg.

Hip Warm-Up 4: Side Leg Swings

Stand in a relaxed, neutral position with your feet about shoulder-width apart.

Stand on one leg and raise the other leg outwards to the side, keeping your leg as straight as possible.

Bring your raised leg across the front of the leg you are standing on towards the other side. Avoid turning your foot sideways by leading with your heel.

You should be achieving a swinging side to side motion with your leg like a pendulum.

Hip Warm-Up 5: forward and Backwards Leg Swings

Stand in a relaxed, neutral position with your feet about shoulder-width apart.

Stand on one leg and raise the other leg forward as far as you can.

Swing your leg backwards as far as you can.

Keep your lower back as still as possible to avoid using your lower back to perform the movement.

When swinging your leg backwards, keep your back as straight as possible and squeeze the glute muscle to pull your leg back.

When swinging your leg forward keep your back straight and contract your core muscles to pull your leg forward.

‰ KNEES

Restricted mobility in your knee joints may cause overuse of the ankles and hips as compensation, leading to pain and problems in those areas.

Knee Warm-Up 1: Flex and Extend

Stand in a relaxed, neutral position with your feet about shoulder-width apart.

Stand on one leg and bend the knee backwards, pulling your heel up towards your bottom before bringing the leg forward to extend and straighten your knee.

Change legs and repeat the exercise with the other knee.

Repeat 10 flexes and extensions in both directions per leg. Repeat five times.

Knee Warm-Up 2: Deep Squats

Stand in a relaxed, neutral position with your feet about shoulder-width apart.

Bend your knees and move into a deep squat position, bringing your bottom as low down to the ground as possible. Make sure that your feet remain flat on the floor and push your weight down through your heels.

Hold this position for one deep breath.

Placing your hands on the floor in front of you, lift your bottom upwards and straighten your legs before lowering yourself into that deep squat position again.

‰ ANKLES

Mobility in the ankles is regularly overlooked but is essential for proper knee joint function. Ankles with good mobility are less prone to sprains and strains, as the ankle stretches more comfortably when accommodating unexpected bending and twisting of the joint.

Ankle Warm-Up 1: Circles

Stand in a relaxed, neutral position with your feet about shoulder-width apart.

Shift your weight to one leg and raise the other so that the tips of your toes are touching the floor.

Rotate your ankle in a clockwise direction, making the circles as big as you can without straining.

Switch directions and rotate in a counterclockwise direction.

Change to your other leg and repeat the exercise.

Be careful not to lean your weight on the rotating ankle to avoid placing too much pressure on the ankle while rotating and causing over stretching.

Ankle Warm-Up 2: Side to Side

Stand in a relaxed, neutral position with your feet about shoulder-width apart.

Shift your weight onto one leg.

Without lifting your foot, roll the ankle of the other leg out to the side. This will cause you to lift the inside edge of your foot and roll your foot over onto the outside edge.

Change direction to roll the inside of your ankle towards your other foot. This will cause you to bring the inside edge of your foot back to the floor, lifting the outside edge, and rolling your foot over onto the inside edge.

Swap over to the other leg and repeat the exercise.

Ankle Warm-Up 3: Flexion and Extension

Stand in a relaxed, neutral position with your feet about shoulder-width apart.

Shift your weight onto one leg and extend the other leg backwards with the tops of your toes resting against the floor.

Keep your knees soft and slightly bent while pushing down on your toes until you feel the stretch up the front of your ankle and shin.

Bring your leg back to the starting position with your foot flat on the floor. Shift your weight onto this leg, bend the knee, and press down on the ball of your foot by bringing your knee forward and down.

Keep your heel flat on the floor and push as far as you can until you feel the stretch up the back of your ankle and calf.

Switch legs and repeat the exercise on the other side.

Perform 10 flexions and 10 extensions per foot. Repeat five times.

MUSCLE WARM-UP EXERCISES

There are three common kettlebell warm-up movement exercises based on the common movements performed during workouts. All of the warm-up exercises are performed without a kettlebell.

Kettlebell Swing

The kettlebell swing warm-up exercise consists of the basic movement pattern used in the swing, high pull, dead lift, and snatch exercises.

Stand in a relaxed, neutral position with your feet about shoulder-width apart.

Bend your knees slightly and bend forward from the hip in a hinge motion while swinging one arm between your legs.

Bring yourself upright, extending through the knees and pushing the hips forward by squeezing the glutes while swinging your arm upwards to chest height.

Unlike performing the kettlebell swing with a kettlebell, you can swing your arm higher, overhead, to help open up the chest.

This replicates the swinging motion of the kettlebell swing and helps to prepare your body to perform the weighted exercise in your workouts.

Glute Bridge

Lay on your back on the floor with your knees bent. It is a good idea to use some form of cushioning like a yoga mat or exercise mat to make the exercise more comfortable.

Place your hands at your sides, palms up, and pull your heels as far in towards your bottom as possible.

Using your core muscles and pushing down through your heels, raise your hips upwards, and squeeze your glute muscles.

Be sure not to employ your lower back muscles, which will cause you to arch your back; also, do not push your weight down through the balls of your feel and lift your heels off the ground.

Lower your hips to the floor just long enough to touch the ground before raising them up again.

Kettlebell Squat

The kettlebell squat warm up exercise consists of the basic movement pattern used in the racked squat, goblet squat, and deck squat exercises.

Stand in a relaxed, neutral position with your feet a little bit wider than shoulder-width apart.

Place your weight on your heels, bend your knees and lower yourself into a squat position.

While lowering yourself into the squat position, keep your chest up and look forward.

Try to bring your thighs parallel to the ground if you can. If you cannot get parallel, drop down as far as you can and work on improving flexibility and joint mobility.

Raise yourself to a standing position again and push your hips forward by squeezing the glute muscles.

Kettlebell Lunge

The kettlebell lunge warm-up exercise consists of the basic movement pattern used in the side lunge, racked lunge, and double lunge exercises.

Stand in a relaxed, neutral position with your feet about shoulder-width apart.

Step backwards with one leg and lower your back knee to the floor while bending your front knee, as if you were moving into a single-leg kneeling position.

Don't drop your knee onto the floor too hard, it should just lightly touch the floor. If you are unable to perform such a deep lunge at first, go as deep as you can and work on your strength and flexibility until you can perform a full deep lunge.

Ensure that both knees are bent at 90-degree angles and that your kneeling and non-kneeling legs are perpendicular to each other at a 90-degree angle at the hips.

Keep your chest up.

Return to the starting position and repeat on the other side.

Hip Opener

Start in a push up or plank position with your hands relatively close together and arms straight.

From that position, bring one leg forward, bend the knee and place your foot flat on the ground next to you, about where your hands are.

Breathe out and as you do so, lower your hips toward the floor, this will cause your other knee to drop towards the floor.

Breathe in as you move your leg back and resume the push up or plank position.

Repeat on the other side.

WEIGHTED KETTLEBELL WARM UP EXERCISES

The previous warm-up exercises are performed without a kettlebell. Now it's time to warm-up using a kettlebell.

Slingshot Warm Up

Stand in a relaxed, neutral position with your feet about shoulder-width apart and your kettlebell in front of you.

Pick up your kettlebell in your right hand and begin to swing it around the front of your body to the left. Pass the kettlebell from your right hand to your left hand.

Continue swinging the kettlebell around the back of your body where you will pass it back from your left hand to your right hand.

Change directions and perform the exercise the other way around.

Halo Warm-Up

Stand in a relaxed, neutral position with your feet about shoulder-width apart and your kettlebell in front of you.

Pick your kettlebell up by the sides of the handles, or horns, and flip it upside down so that the body of the kettlebell is facing upwards. Lift it to chest height.

From there, raise your kettlebell to head height and rotate it in a clockwise circle around your head.

Change directions and perform the exercise again.

Kettlebell Good Morning Exercise

Stand in a relaxed, neutral position with your feet about shoulder-width apart and your kettlebell in front of you.

Pick up your kettlebell by placing your hands on the sides of the handle, thumbs around the inside of the handle, palms facing you, and backs of the hands facing forward.

Lift it slowly and carefully over one shoulder.

Once the kettlebell is behind you, slide your hands to the top corners of the handle and let it come to rest gently against your back between your shoulder blades.

Keep your elbows close together and your knees soft.

Hinge your hips backward as if sticking your bottom out, pushing your weight through your heels, and lean your torso forward until you feel the stretch in your hamstrings at the backs of your legs.

Be mindful to keep your back flat, don't arch your lower back and don't round your upper back and shoulders.

Bring yourself upright to a standing position, squeezing the glutes.

Breathe out as you bend forward and in again as you straighten up.

WARM-UP ROUTINE

WARM-UP EXERCISE	REPS
Neck Warm-Up 1: Ear to Shoulder	3 reps per side
Neck Warm-Up 2: Look Left to Right	3 reps in each direction
Neck Warm-Up 3: Chin Up and	3 resp

Down	
Neck Warm-Up 4: Neck Rolls	3 reps in each direction
Shoulder Warm-Up 1: Backwards and forward Shoulder Circles	5 reps per arm in each direction. Repeat 3 times.
Shoulder Warm-Up 2: Lasso Overhead	5 reps per arm in each direction. Repeat 3 times.
Shoulder Warm-Up 3: Inward and Outward Rotations	5 reps per arm in each direction. Repeat 3 times.
Shoulder Warm-Up 4: Self-Hugs	15 reps
Shoulder Warm-Up 5: Shoulder Rolls	5 reps in each direction. Repeat 3 times.

Upper Back Warm-Up 1: Rotations	5 reps in each direction. Repeat 3 times.
Upper Back Warm-Up 2: Lateral Reaches	5 reps in each direction. Repeat 3 times.
Upper Back 3: Opening the Chest	15 reps

Elbow Warm-Up 1: Flex and Extend	5 reps per arm. Repeat 5 times. OR 15 reps with both arms simultaneously
Elbow Warm-Up 2: Elbow Lassos	5 reps per arm in each direction. Repeat 3 times.

Wrist Warm-Up 1:	5 reps per movement.

Rotations, Backwards and forward, Side to Side	Repeat 3 times.
Wrist Warm-Up 2: Wrist Extensions	5 reps in each direction. Repeat 3 times.
Hip Warm-Up 1: Circles	5 reps in each direction. Repeat 3 times
Hip Warm-Up 2: Side to side, Backwards and forward	5 reps in each direction. Repeat 3 times.
Hip Warm-Up 3: Leg Circles	5 reps per leg in each direction. Repeat 3 times.
Hip Warm-Up 4: Side Leg Swings	5 swing reps per leg. Repeat 3 times.
Hip Warm-Up 5:	5 swing reps per leg.

forward and Backwards Leg Swings	Repeat 3 times.
Knee Warm-Up 1: Flex and Extend	5 reps per leg. Repeat 3 times.
Knee Warm-Up 2: Deep Squats	15 reps
Ankle Warm-Up 1: Circles	5 reps per foot in each direction. Repeat 3 times.
Ankle Warm-Up 2: Side to Side	5 reps per foot in each direction. Repeat 3 times.
Ankle Warm-Up 3: Flexion and Extension	5 reps per leg. Repeat 3 times.

Kettlebell Swing	15 reps per side
Glute Bridge	10 to 20 reps
Kettlebell Squat	15 reps
Kettlebell Lunge	10 reps per side
Hip Opener	10 reps per side
Slingshot Warm-Up	10 to 20 reps in each direction
Halo Warm-Up	5 to 10 reps in each direction
Kettlebell Good Morning Exercise	10 reps

IMPORTANT NOTE:

Warming up is incredibly important. Start by working through the joint warm-up exercises to get your joints moving. Pay attention to joints that exhibit poor mobility. If you find that some joints need some extra work, spend more time focusing on improving mobility in those joints and a little less time warming up the others. However, don't completely neglect joints that already have good mobility, all your joints need to be warmed up before a workout.

Follow through with the non-weighted warm-up exercises to get your body moving by replicating the common movements used in kettlebell training. Once you are loosened up, you can introduce a kettlebell and perform the weighted exercises.

From start to finish, your entire workout should only take about 10 to 15 minutes. It is a great opportunity to become aware of areas that need work and get your head into the game before your workout. If you are not feeling particularly well, a good warm-up can be used as a light and easy workout instead of skipping your workout altogether.

Chapter 9: Kettlebell Workouts For Beginners

If you ask any trainer, they will tell you that kettlebell is here to stay because they have outstanding fitness and postural benefits. It is the one workout technique that can work multiple joints all at the same time. It is the one technique that you can use to achieve so many results simultaneously. It is not only great for the heart and the core but also offers the ability to stabilize the body.

To warm up the body with this exercise, begin by standing with your feet such that your feet are hip-width apart. Hold the kettlebell to your chest and then using your right hand, hold the corner of the kettlebell handle and lower down into a squat position. Once you are on the squat position, begin to thread the bell in between your legs so that you reach behind and use your left hand to grip the corner of the handle.

Now that the kettlebell is in your left hand behind your left leg start moving it along the outer parts of your left thigh. Then start threading it back to the middle of your legs but this time, ensure that you grab it with your right hand and hold it behind your right leg. Again, start moving it around the right leg and then bring it to the front of your right hand. As a beginner, you can start with at least five reps and then work your way up to 10 gradually once the body can handle it.

1. Kettlebell Swing

This is one of the most popular workout exercises that you should incorporate into your daily fitness routine. To get the perfect kettlebell swing, start by standing over the kettlebell with your feet hips apart and your chest up.

Hold your shoulders back and then move down with the kettlebell lined between your feet. It is important that you invest a kettlebell that permits you to swing using one of the perfect techniques without having to challenge yourself. If you are a beginner, it is critical that you start with a lightweight kettlebell or use one that is way lighter than what you are used to.

Now, squat down while ensuring that you grip the kettlebell with your palms such that your thumb loosely grips around the handle. Stand tall while gripping onto the kettlebell. It is critical that you keep your arms long and loose enough to engage the core and the cause the shoulder blades to retract.

At this point, it is important that you start shifting the bodyweight towards your heels while keeping the knees softened. Then slowly lower the rear end towards the wall behind you and then start swinging the kettlebell.

Start driving your heels so that your quads are engaged while still swinging the kettlebell. It is critical that as you swing the kettlebell, it reaches your chest and the arms remain extended. As the bell begins to come downwards, allow the weight to work the magic while you get ready for the next rep.

Shift the weight towards your heels so that the glutes and the hamstrings are loaded and then the weight will move behind your legs. While the bells transition from the back to the front, keep engaging your heels and your hips to maximize the benefits. Repeat the whole process at least ten times, and once you can handle it, you can gradually increase the reps.

2. Turkish Get Up

This is one of the most commonly known full body workout that integrates fundamental movement patterns that are important in conditioning the stabilizer muscles and the core throughout the process.

It is termed the best stabilizing exercises and has been used for so many decades in ancient Greek. It is believed that the Greek would not train a boy until they can get off the floor while holding the weights above their heads. This exercise entails seven stages;

Stage 1

Start by forming a fetal position while ensuring that you are holding the kettlebell. Then roll onto your back and then hold the bell such that your arm is straightened out. Fix your gaze on the kettlebell and ensure that your eyes are not taken off it.

Stage 2

Start bending your leg so that they are in the same direction as the kettlebell. At the same time, place your opposite arm such that it is at 45 degrees.

Stage 3

Once you are seated along the line of your arm, crush the handle to your elbow and then follow up with the hand. Start to position the kettlebell arm in its rightful socket in such a way that the shoulders are positioned away from the ear.

Stage 4

Now, start pushing from the heel of your bent leg and then push your hips up so that they are fully extended. Ensure that there is a straight line running from the bottom hand to the bell.

Stage 5

Sweep the straight leg through and then back so that you are in half kneeling position.

Stage 6

Lift the hands off the floor and then begin to extend the body so that it is straight.

Take your eyes off the bell and focus on what lies ahead of you.

Stage 7

Drive slowly from your heel and stand up straight on your feet. Once you achieve stability, you can reverse the movements and start from the beginning to the end for the number of replicates that is desired.

3. Kettlebell Windmill

This is an exercise that is designed mainly for strengthening the core. It also plays a central role in decreasing waistline. Start by positioning the kettlebell at the front of your lead foot. Use your opposite arm to press overhead.

Clean the bell to your shoulder by simply extending through your hips and the legs such that the kettlebell moves in the direction of your shoulders. Start rotating the wrist in such a way that the palms face forward and then press the kettlebell overhead by simply extending the elbows straight.

In this position, ensure that you keep the kettlebell locked out so that you can now push your glutes in the same direction as the locked bell. Extend your feet to achieve a 45-degree angle from the arm while maintaining the kettlebell locked out.

While you bend the hips, begin to slowly lean forward until you reach the ground with your free hands. While doing this, it is important that you keep your eyes gazing on the kettlebell throughout as you hold it over your head. Take a 30-second pause once you reach the floor before you can get back to your starting position.

4. Single Leg Deadlift

This exercise is important in helping you learn how to stabilize when in motion. It is critical that you practice this movement so that when you are holding a kettlebell, you can swing it at high speed without tripping. It is a comprehensive exercise that plays a critical role in singling out your legs during the deadlift process.

One thing that you have to bear in mind when engaging in this exercise is that it requires balance. It is also essential that you pay attention to your glutes, hamstrings and your lower back. Indeed, it is a great exercise that will help you achieve toned lean legs while strengthening your posterior chain.

The first thing that you have to do is position your feet together while you place the kettlebells on your toes. Then pick it up while you raise one leg and the other behind you. Maintain a straight back as you place the bell back to the floor and repeat the whole process for about 5-10 reps.

One of the safety tips that should help you as you engage in this workout is to hold on to the kettlebell handle tight while maintaining a tight core. As you do this, you should be able to feel the tension on both your hamstrings and glutes.

5. Kettlebell Goblet Squat

The first thing that you do here is to hold the kettlebells by the horns and then drive your shoulder blades towards each other and downwards towards the chest so that the chest opens. Then tuck your elbows in so that your forearms are in a vertical orientation.

Stand with both your feet wider than hip-width apart. Ensure that the feet are slightly turned out and then take in deep breaths into your belly. Start twisting your feet into the ground and take a squatting position while keeping your torso upright. Go as low as possible without allowing your tailbone to tuck under your butt.

6. One-arm Overhead Press

Start by standing tall while holding the kettlebell in one hand at the level of your shoulder. Stand firmly with your feet rooted into the ground as though you were getting ready to resist a push. Take in deep breaths into your belly and ensure that you brace your glutes and abs.

Now pull your ribs down so that your spine looks elongated and your chest is out, and the tailbone is slightly tilted. Start pressing the weight overhead. It is important that you ensure your chin is pulled back so that the weight clears it easily. Now lower the kettlebell by pulling it back into position as though you were performing a pull-up.

It is important that you do not get fixated on getting the overhead lockout immediately. You have to understand that achieving that right-angle elbow bend is not easy for most people. Therefore, if you see the need to arch your back so that your ribs can flare, do it.

This will help you lockout the arms overhead so that the shoulders train effectively. In most cases, you might find it necessary to regress the movements towards the ground by simply lying down on the floor with your triceps against it. Then press upwards from there as though you were doing a bench press only this time with a shortened range of motion.

7. Kettlebell Deadlift

Start this exercise by placing the kettlebells on the floor in between your feet. Now stand with your feet at hip-width apart. Slightly bend the knees so that you can push your butt back. Ensure that your feet are rooted to the ground while you try to lower your torso until your arms can grip onto the kettlebell handle.

With your chest out, keep your lower back naturally arched as possible. It is important that you let your eyes gaze in front of you but slightly lower. Then grasp the kettlebell using both your hands and then take a deep breath into your belly. Now drive through your heels and lift the bells while you extend your hips to lockout.

8.Kettlebell One-arm Row

Start by placing the kettlebell down on the floor and then place your right foot in front as you take a staggered stance. Plant your foot right outside your weight.

Ensure that you plant the ball of your left foot into the ground and fold it at the hips as you bring yourself into a sitting position in such a way that your butt and

torso are at a 45-degree angle to the ground. Then rest your elbow on your right thigh for support. Then reach out for the kettlebell with the help of your left hand.

Inhale in slowly into your belly as you draw your shoulders back and towards each other. Brace your core as you row the weight towards your hips. Squeeze your shoulder blades together at the top and repeat the whole process for about 8-10 reps.

9. Kettlebell Goblet Half Get Up

Just like the kettlebell swing workout, so many people who use kettlebells prefer to skip ahead to moves that are more advanced. Instead of jumping right in with the Turkish get up which is quite complex, it is important that you understand that as a beginner, starting with half get up still offers you incredible core workout just like any other flexibility workout.

To do this, start by lying down on your back while holding the kettlebells by the horns. Inhale in softly into the belly while you brace your abs. Now, start performing sit-ups as you tuck your right foot towards your butt and then slide your left foot behind

you in such a way that you form something like a "shin box" while on the floor. Ensure that both knees are bent at a right angle with both your feet facing away from each other.

Extend your hips as though you are bringing yourself to a standing position and then bring your left foot to the front again. Plant it to the ground so that the knee is at a right angle. Then turn the hind leg so that it points directly behind you as you finish on a lunge position. Reverse the whole motion as you come down to a lying position on the ground.

10. Kettlebell Halo

One of the things that is important to note is that as you brace your body in the correct orientation while you change the position of the kettlebells, you have to stay alert and comfortable. Move the kettlebells in a circular motion around the body to form something like a halo. This will strengthen the core and prepare you for more rigorous exercises down the line. It also plays a critical role in exposing weaknesses as well as a lack of balance.

If you are not able to hand off the kettlebells behind you, there is a high chance that you will not be able to reach your buttock as

well. Therefore, if you are going to do the most basic shoulder halo, it is advisable that you stand with both your feet so that they are in between the hip and are shoulder-width apart. Hold the kettlebells upside down by the horns such that the bell faces upwards. Then root your feet to the ground as you draw your ribs down.

Begin to move the kettlebells around your head while ensuring that you keep an upright posture by not bending the torso in any direction. Now, start moving slowly to avoid hitting your head and make full circles while alternating the orientation.

11. Kettlebell Clean

This is a very important exercise that targets the back, the glutes, and the hamstrings. Begin this exercise with the kettlebell on the floor. Ensure that it is positioned slightly in front of you in such a way that it lies in between your legs and at shoulder-width apart. Now, slightly bend your knees and hinge at the hips as you grasp the kettlebell. Then pull it back in between your legs using one hand such that the thumb points backward. This creates momentum.

Start driving your hips forward and keep your back as straightened as possible. This will help in initiating the upward movement of the kettlebells. Once the kettlebell goes above the height of the bellybutton, pull it back gently so that you can slide your fist around and under the bell. It will nestle softly at the back of your wrist, and this is referred to as the rack position. Finally, push the kettlebell out and allow it to swing down in between your legs. Repeat the whole process for three repetitions if you are a beginner.

It is important to note that, this exercise is even-handed. This means that you have to do equal amounts of repetitions on both sides to avoid developing injuries and imbalances. If you are new to this exercise, you will realize that it is more overpowering than the clean which essentially causes the bell to flip over and cause a bang on the wrist.

Rather than opening your hand, it is advisable that you focus so that you get it around the bell to avoid causing it to flip so that you can efficiently get the weight to the rack position without any pain. Ensure that your trajectory is straight; therefore, do not swing the kettlebell to the right or left. Instead, swing the kettlebell up and pull the bell up and back towards you. Allow your lower body to perform most of the work in getting the bell in its rightful place.

12.   Kettlebell Pistol Squat

When doing kettlebell exercises, there is so much demand placed on the knee, hips and ankle mobility while also requiring that they maintain stability during lifting. Considering that the pistol is purely a unilateral exercise of the legs, there is a high chance that any gap in movement is taken into account leading you to your weaknesses.

This means that you have to master the pistol by training your weak points so that you stay safe, strong and perform better at deadlifting, sprinting, cleaning and squatting. In short, all these translate to your overall performance.

One of the greatest benefits of learning the pistol squat is boosting the mobility of the ankle. This is the movement that comes about when you pull your toes in the direction of your knees, when you have better dorsiflexion, the tibia, and the knee to move forward over the toes without necessarily causing the knees to rise above the ground.

To do this exercise, start by picking up the kettlebell using both your hands. Hold it against your chest but slightly below your neck region. Now, move one leg and then hold it off the ground. With the other leg, start to squat down as you bend one knee.

While you squat down, hold the kettlebell at the front of your chest and maintain that position when you get closer to the floor. Use the force from your heel to push yourself back up so that you return to standing position. Repeat this exercise for about 3-5 reps if you are a beginner.

13. Kettlebell Jerk

This is another overhead ballistic kettlebell lift that utilizes more leg power and less strength on the upper parts of the body compared to a push press. In other words, the kettlebell jerk is a powerful lift that allows one to perform as many reps as possible.

You can even get a heavier weight overhead when performing the kettlebell jerk than when doing the kettlebell push press. It also plays a central role in giving you more cardiorespiratory training. Therefore, in addition to the benefits that you get from the push press, the jerk helps you to lower the stress levels on the shoulder joints by simply engaging more leg power.

It needs more stability on the shoulders for the sake of fixation, and therefore, it has the potential to create incredibly stable

shoulders. As mentioned, it uses lower leg power, and this helps in developing power around the calves which in turn increases the ankle joint stability.

Before you can attempt the jerk, it is important that you master the overhead press and the push press first. This is because it will offer you the opportunity to perfectly get the bell path, train the body to fixate the kettlebell correctly, and practice the dip in a very simple lift. All these techniques are very important when learning the jerk technique. For you to get into the very first dip with your heels, the mobility of the ankles is key.

To catch the kettlebell is to get into a quarter overhead squat position, it is essential that you comfortably get into position with vertical arms. This is because, the exercise is more demanding on the mobility of your upper back, lower back and the shoulders as compared to the overhead lockout position.

The best test is for you to try doing a broomstick overhead squats. If you cannot get to a quarter squat position with vertical arms, then you have lots of mobility work to do before you can perform the kettlebell jerk.

Once you have everything ready, start by holding the kettlebell by the handle. Cling the kettlebell to your shoulders by simply extending your hips and legs as you pull it towards the shoulders. As you do so, ensure that you are rotating your wrist such that your palm faces forward, and this will serve as your starting position.

Now, begin to dip your body by slightly bending the knees while maintaining the torso in an upright posture. Immediately start reversing the direction as you drive through the heels. In other words, you should jump to create momentum. As you do that, press the kettlebell overhead to lockout by extending your arms.

Use the momentum of your body to move the weight. Then receive the weight overhead by returning to a squat position under the weight and keep the weight overhead before you can return to a standing position. Lower the weight and repeat the whole process for about 3-5 reps if you are a beginner.

Conclusion

Kettlebells have been around for much longer than we realize, they have humble origins and a big future ahead of them in the world of fitness and competitive sport. As kettlebells have become a household name in gyms and fitness studios, so too are women learning about the benefits of strength training.

Long gone are the days when the ladies would shy away from the heavy lifting; these days we step up to the plate and show the boys who's boss. Women all around the world are doing it and you can too. The best part is that you will not only lose weight training with kettlebells, it's also tons of fun!

Kettlebells are growing in popularity among women who want to get strong, fit, and lean and it's no surprise why. They are extremely versatile, offering you a whole arsenal of effective exercises in the battle against the bulge. These exercises are proven to be fat-busting moves, burning up to 400 calories in just 20 minutes and working up to 600 muscles in a single workout. There is no other single workout tool that can offer you such versatility with limited space and time and with an affordable price tag.

Working with kettlebells provides you with high-intensity workouts that only take a short amount of time to complete with maximum fat burning results. They are compact, requiring little space to use, and they're portable so you can take them anywhere and train at any time. You don't ever need to set foot in a gym, you can do it all from the comfort of your own home. Kettlebells officially give you no excuse to skip a workout or put off starting.

This is your chance to make a positive change, a change for yourself, an investment in yourself. When you pick up a kettlebell, you are forming a life-long love affair with your health, fitness, and body. Whatever your goals are, kettlebells will help you get there and make you look good along the way. These age-old strength training tools have changed not only my life but the lives of countless women across the glow. Now you can change your life too by using the information I've provided in this book to start your journey to a happier, healthier, and slimmer you.

Thank you for allowing me to share my passion and knowledge with you. I'm thrilled that you have taken the time to read this book which has been written as my way of helping you reach your weight loss goals. Now it's time to start shopping for your new best friend, a new kettlebell, and start your journey today.

Don't forget to leave a review of your experience of reading Kettlebells for Women!

CPSIA information can be obtained
at www.ICGtesting.com
Printed in the USA
BVHW032307160822
644778BV00008B/77

9 781990 268618